RAMADAN
CUT AND PASTE
WORKBOOK FOR PRESCHOOL

By MezzyArt Designs

FOR MORE VISIT US AT: **https://www.amazon.com/author/mezzyartdesigns**

THIS BOOK BELONGS TO:

....

RAMADAN CUTTING PRACTICE

RAMADAN CUTTING PRACTICE

Color, Cut and Paste Ramadan Fun Faces!

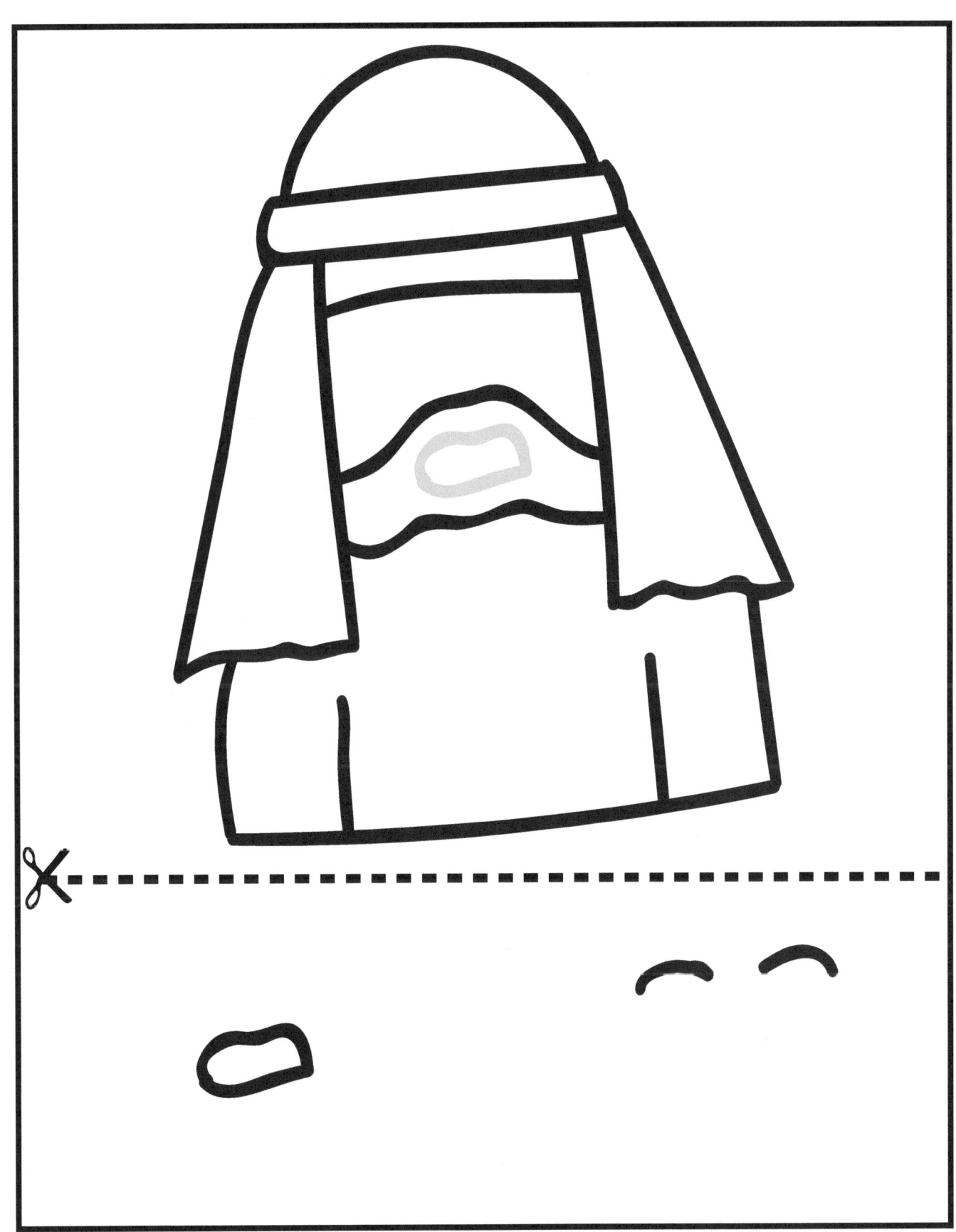

Color, Cut and Paste Ramadan Fun Faces!

Color, Cut and Paste Ramadan Fun Faces!

RAMADAN COUNTING

Count, Color, Cut and Paste the Right Number!

Count, Color, Cut and Paste the Right Number!

What Picture Comes Next?
Color them all!

What Picture Comes Next?
Color them all!

RAMADAN SHADOW MATCH
Cut, Color and Paste pictures that match their shadows

RAMADAN SHADOW MATCH

RAMADAN SHADOW MATCH

Cut, Color and Paste pictures that match their shadows

RAMADAN SHADOW MATCH

Cut, Color and Paste pictures that match their shadows

RAMADAN SHADOW MATCH

Cut, Color and Paste pictures that match their shadows

SMALLEST TO BIGGEST

Color, Cut and Paste them in Order of smallest to biggest.

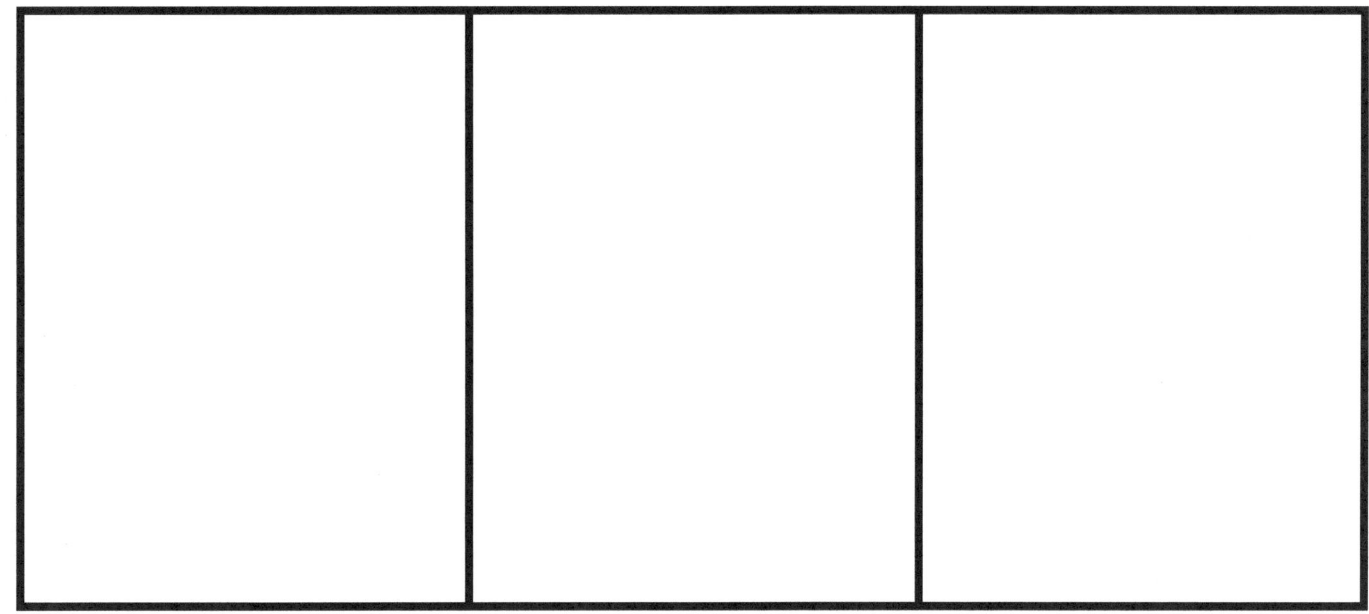

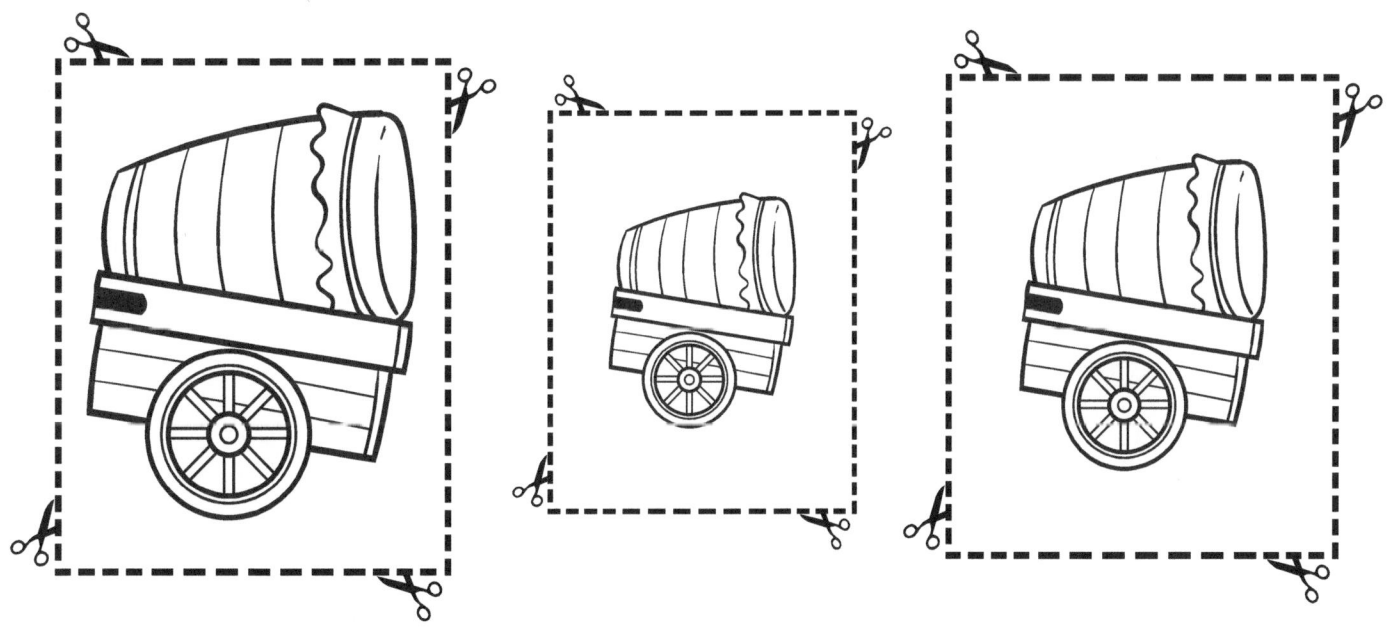

Color, Cut and Paste them in Order or smallest to biggest

BIGGEST TO SMALLEST

Color, Cut and Paste them in Order of smallest to biggest.

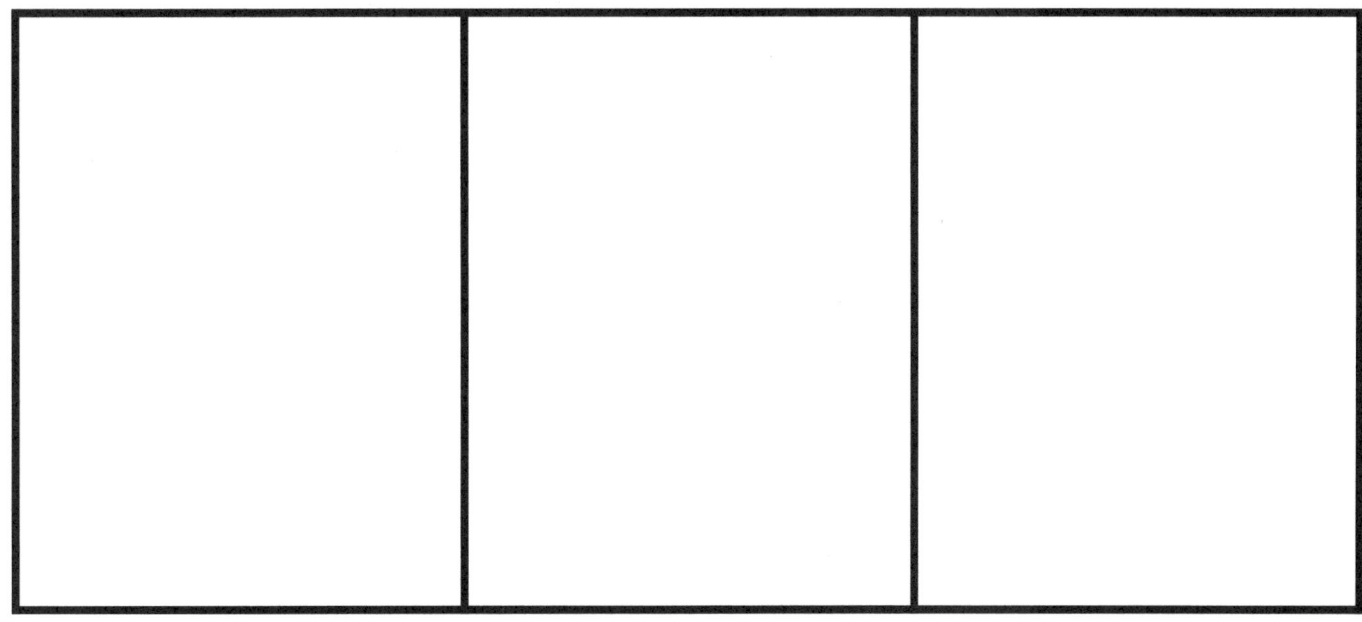

RAMADAN COLORING
COLOR AND CUT!

RAMADAN COLORING
COLOR AND CUT!

RAMADAN COLORING
COLOR AND CUT!

RAMADAN COLORING
COLOR AND CUT!

RAMADAN COLORING
COLOR AND CUT!

RAMADAN COLORING
COLOR AND CUT!

RAMADAN COLORING
COLOR AND CUT!

RAMADAN COLORING
COLOR AND CUT!

RAMADAN COLORING
COLOR AND CUT!

Ramadan Kareem

17610670R00031